HEINEMANN STATE STUDIES

Uniquely
Missouri

Lisa Owens

Heinemann Library
Chicago, Illinois

© 2004 Heinemann Library
a division of Reed Elsevier Inc.
Chicago, Illinois

Customer Service   888-454-2279

Visit our website at www.heinemannlibrary.com

Designed by Heinemann Library
Printed in China by WKT Company Limited.

07 06 05 04
10 9 8 7 6 5 4 3 2 1

**Library of Congress
Cataloging-in-Publication Data**

Owens, Lisa, 1965–
  Uniquely Missouri / Lisa Owens.
    p. cm.—(Heinemann state studies)
Summary: Provides an overview of various aspects
of Missouri that make it a unique state, including
its people, land, culture, and attractions.

Includes bibliographical references and index.
  ISBN 1-4034-4495-1 (lib. bdg.)—
ISBN 1-4034-4510-9 (pbk.)
  1. Missouri—Juvenile literature. [1. Missouri.]
I. Title. II. Series.
  F466.3.O94 2003

                              2003009413

Acknowledgments

Development and photo research by
BOOK BUILDERS LLC

The author and publishers are grateful to the
following for permission to reproduce copyright
material:

Cover photographs by (top, L-R): Buddy Mays/
Corbis; Dave G. Houser/Corbis; Office of the
Secretary of State; Kelly-Mooney Photography/
Corbis; (main) Owaki-Kulla/Corbis.

Title page: Missouri Division of Tourism; Contents
page: Missouri Division of Tourism; pp. 5T, 7T, 7B,
11B, 12T, 14T, 14B, 15T, 15BR, 18, 20BR, 28, 29, 31,
35, 36, 38 Missouri Division of Tourism; pp. 5B, 24,
25 Andre Jenny/Alamy; pp. 8, 41, 45 maps by IMA
for Book Builders LLC; p. 9 Alamy; p. 10 Gerrit Bunt-
rock/Anthony Blake Photo Library/Alamy; p. 11T
Office of the Secretary of State; p. 12B David Boag/
Alamy; pp. 20ML, 21B, 22TR Popperfoto/Alamy;
p. 21T Bettmann/Corbis; p. 22BL AFP/Corbis; p. 23
Ernest Haas/Hulton Getty; p. 26 Tim Bommel,
Missouri House of Representatives; p. 30 Craig
Brown/Index Stock/Alamy; p. 32 Martin Jacobs/Food
Pix/Getty; p. 34 illustration by R. Capozzeli for
Heinemann; p. 39 Buddy Mays/Corbis; p. 40
Dave G. Houser/Corbis; p. 42T Owaki-Kulla/Corbis;
p. 42B Hulton Getty; p. 43 Courtesy Museum of
Westward Expansion/Courtesy of Missouri Division
of Tourism; p. 44 Kelly-Mooney Photography/Corbis.

Special thanks to Steve Potts of the University of
Nebraska for his expert advice on the preparation
of this book on his neighboring state.

Every effort has been made to contact copyright
holders of any material reproduced in this book.
Any omissions will be rectified in subsequent
printings if notice is given to the publisher.

Cover Pictures

Top (left to right) Branson, Mark Twain's
boyhood home in Hannibal, Missouri state
flag, Clydesdale horse **Main** Gateway Arch
in St. Louis

Some words are shown in bold, **like this.**
You can find out what they mean by looking
in the glossary.

Contents

Uniquely Missouri

Welcome to Missouri, home to some of the most unique attractions, events, and individuals in the United States. Unique means that something is special and also difficult to find anywhere else. Among the many unique things discussed in this book are Missouri's more than 1,450 caves and the first Olympic Games ever held in the United States.

WHAT DOES *MISSOURI* MEAN?

During the 1600s the Native American Fox culture hunted in the area that would later become Missouri. They used the word *Missouri* to name their enemy, another Native American tribe—a branch of the Sioux—in the area. The word means "people with big canoes" in the Fox language. Eventually, Missouri was adopted as the name of the area's major river and the state itself.

MAJOR MISSOURI CITIES

Missouri's capital is Jefferson City. It is located along the Missouri River near the center of the state. It was named capital of Missouri in 1826. It was a small settlement then, but the town grew during the 1830s when it became a popular stopping point for steamboats and stagecoaches. Today Jefferson City is still small, with a population of about 40,000. The city's biggest employer is the state government, whose home is at the state capitol. Visitors like to stop by the white limestone capitol building to see the **murals** depicting Missouri history on display.

Kansas City is located near the state's western border along the Missouri River. It is Missouri's most populous

city. It has about 442,000 people. Originally, Kansas City was two towns, Kansas and Westport. Kansas formed around a fur-trading post in the 1820s. Westport started at about the same time as home to the area's cowboys. The two communities combined to form Kansas City in 1899. Today, Kansas City is an agricultural force. Hogs, cattle, wheat, corn, and soybeans are grown on the farmland surrounding the city.

The J. C. Nichols Fountain on Country Club Plaza was named for the man who created Kansas City's downtown plaza district.

Kansas City is also known for producing such varied products as greeting cards and frozen dinners.

Two French fur traders founded St. Louis, located on Missouri's eastern border, in 1764. They named St. Louis for Louis IX, who was the king of France from 1226 to 1270. St. Louis is the state's largest **metropolitan** area. Its major business is airplane manufacturing. Music has played a big part in the city's history. The musical style known as the St. Louis **blues** was first heard in the early 1900s. It is a mixture of jazz, blues, and **ragtime.**

St. Louis's Gateway Arch, pictured in the background, was designed to last 1,000 years.

Missouri's Geography and Climate

The variations in Missouri's landscape and climate help contribute to many of the state's most unique geographical features.

MISSOURI'S GEOGRAPHY

Missouri is in the midwestern region of the United States. It is located on both the Missouri and Mississippi rivers—the two longest rivers in the United States. Missouri ranks as the nineteenth largest state in terms of area. Its borders are formed by Iowa to the north; Illinois, Kentucky, and Tennessee to the east; Arkansas to the south; and Nebraska, Kansas, and Oklahoma to the west.

Missouri has four main geographic areas. From north to south, they are the Dissected Till Plains, the Osage Plains, the Ozark Plateau, and the Mississippi Alluvial Plain.

The Dissected Till Plains area is north of the Missouri River. It contains **fertile** farmland. The area is considered a **prairie,** and it includes many rivers and streams.

The mostly flat Osage Plains are found in western Missouri. Hundreds of years ago, the plains were primarily grasslands, but over time fires brought on by severe drought destroyed much of the grass. The soil here is less fertile than in the Dissected Till Plains. However, it is good for growing corn and soybeans.

The Ozark Plateau is the state's largest land area. It is known for its variations in **terrain.** There are forests, caves, low mountains, rivers, lakes, and springs. The highest point in Missouri, Taum Sauk Mountain, is found in the Ozark Plateau. It is found in the St. Francois Mountains in Iron County and measures 1,772 feet above sea level.

The Mississippi Alluvial Plain spans the southern part of Missouri. The region was once swampland, but the water was drained in the early 1900s to create fertile farmland. The southeastern section of Missouri that cuts into Arkansas is called the Boot Heel because it resembles a boot's heel. The lowest point in Missouri is found here. It is in the St. Francis River near Arbyrd and is 230 feet above sea level.

Missouri's Climate

Missouri has four distinct seasons each year—a cold winter, a mild and often rainy spring, a warm and humid summer, and a crisp, cool fall. The average July temperature in the state is 78°F, but because of the high **humidity** in Missouri, the temperature seems much warmer. The average January temperature is about 30°F.

Precipitation is any moisture that makes its way from the sky to the ground. Missouri experiences all types of precipitation. The state's yearly precipitation rate ranges from 30 inches in the northwest to 50 inches in the southeast.

Taum Sauk Mountain State Park contains nearly 7,500 acres of unspoiled wilderness.

The coldest temperature ever recorded in Missouri was –40°F on February 13, 1905, in Warsaw.

Extreme Weather: Tornadoes

A tornado is a powerful funnel of spinning air that shoots down to the earth from a **cumulonimbus cloud.** Missouri is part of what weather forecasters call Tornado Alley in the United States. Other states in Tornado Alley are Kansas, Oklahoma, and Texas. The largest number of tornadoes and the most dangerous ones in the world happen in Tornado Alley, usually between March and July. This region experiences up to 700 tornadoes per year.

Most of the precipitation in Missouri is concentrated in the southern part of the state.

Average Annual Precipitation Missouri

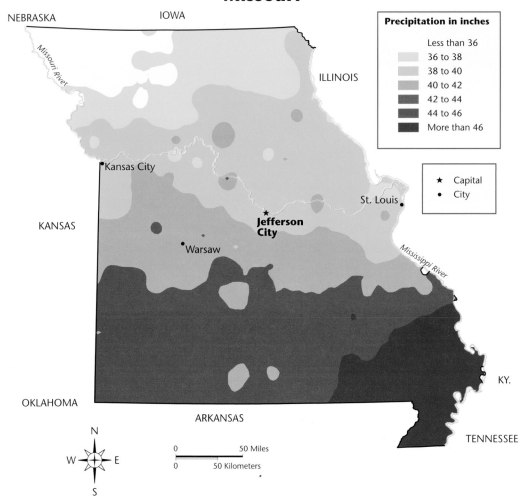

Precipitation in inches

Less than 36
36 to 38
38 to 40
40 to 42
42 to 44
44 to 46
More than 46

★ Capital
• City

Famous Firsts

ST. LOUIS WORLD'S FAIR FIRSTS

There was much to see and do at the St. Louis World's Fair of 1904. About twenty million people from all over the world visited this six-month-long event in Missouri. They saw exhibits of art, technology, culture, and many famous firsts. For example, iced tea was served at the World's Fair before it was served anywhere else in the world. Nobody was interested in buying hot drinks during the hot summer months of the fair. So Richard Blechyden of the Far East Tea House decided to serve the tea over ice. His invention quickly became the most popular drink at the fair.

Another big first at the fair was the first Olympic Games ever held in the United States. Events at the 1904 St. Louis Olympics included swimming, running, and rock throwing. Athletes from all over the world competed, including the first African Americans ever to take part in the games. Also, it was the first Olympics at which gold, silver, and bronze medals were given to the top three athletes in each event.

The St. Louis World's Fair showcased more than 1,500 buildings, including some that visitors can still tour today.

About one-third of all U.S. families eat at least a gallon of ice cream every two weeks.

The ice-cream cone also made its first-ever appearance at the fair. Teenage ice-cream vendor Arnold Fornichou ran out of the paper dishes he used to serve his ice cream. He needed to solve his problem, and fast. While watching Syrian vendor Ernest Hamwi make wafer-thin waffles, Fornichou figured out what to do. Soon, with Hamwi's help, he was serving his ice cream in rolled-up waffles. These were the world's first ice-cream cones.

EDUCATION FIRSTS

In another first for Missouri, Saint Louis University (SLU) received its formal **charter** from the state in 1832. This made it the oldest university west of the Mississippi River. In 1843 SLU also opened the first law school west of the Mississippi.

In 1873 the St. Louis Board of Education opened the first public-school kindergarten in the United States. And in 1908 the University of Missouri at Columbia opened the world's first school of **journalism.**

OTHER FIRSTS

The world's first parachute jump from an airplane occurred in St. Louis. Captain Albert Berry made the jump on March 1, 1912, landing at Jefferson Barracks, a military site. The parachute, made out of a hot air balloon, safely carried Berry 1,500 feet from the plane to the ground.

In 1889 the Pearl Milling Company of St. Joseph, Missouri, introduced Aunt Jemima Pancake Mix. This was the first **ready-mix** food ever to be sold in U.S. stores. The mix is still sold in stores today.

Missouri's State Symbols

MISSOURI STATE FLAG

Missouri adopted its state flag in 1913. The 24 stars that surround the state seal in the center of the flag symbolize Missouri's admittance to the Union as its 24th state.

MISSOURI STATE SEAL

The Great Seal of the State of Missouri was adopted on January 11, 1822. Like the stars on the flag, the 24 stars at the top of the seal represent Missouri's entry into the United States as the 24th state. The two grizzly bears standing on a scroll of the state motto symbolize Missourians' strength and bravery. The bears hold a shield bordered with the words "United We Stand, Divided We Fall." This saying illustrates that Missouri is proud to be part of the United States. The Missouri bear and the silver crescent moon in the center symbolize the state at the time of the seal's creation—a state in which wealth would grow like the crescent moon grows to a full moon. The eagle clutching arrows represents the United States.

The Missouri state flag features bold red, white, and blue stripes—symbols of the state's loyalty to the Union.

The Roman numeral MDCCCXX on the state seal stands for the year 1820, when Missouri wrote its state constitution.

MISSOURI STATE MOTTO

A motto is a saying that means something special to the people who use it. For Missourians, the state motto is a code by which they live. The motto is "The welfare of the people shall be the supreme law." It means that the good of the people guides the state.

STATE NICKNAME: SHOW ME STATE

Missouri's best-known nickname is the "Show Me State." It appears on state license plates. Missouri congressman Willard Duncan Vandiver is usually thought to have used the phrase in 1899, explaining that he, like other Missourians, wanted to hear the plain and simple truth.

Festivals throughout Missouri hold fiddlers' contests each year.

STATE MUSICAL INSTRUMENT: FIDDLE

The fiddle was named Missouri's state musical instrument in 1987. Fiddle music has been common at family gatherings and community events in Missouri for more than 100 years.

STATE FLOWER: WHITE HAWTHORN

On March 16, 1923, the white hawthorn was named the official Missouri state flower. It is common all over the state and sprouts clusters of white blossoms in April and May.

The hawthorn flower is found on about 75 hawthorn tree varieties throughout Missouri.

"Missouri Waltz"

Hush-a-bye, ma baby, slumber time is comin' soon;
Rest yo' head upon my breast, while mommy hums a tune;
The sandman is callin', where shadows are fallin',
While the soft breezes sigh as in days long gone by.

Way down in Missouri where I heard this melody,
When I was a little child on my mommy's knee;
The old folks were hummin', their banjos were strummin'
So sweet and low.

Strum, strum, strum, strum, strum,
Seems I hear those banjos playin' once again,
Hum, hum, hum, hum, hum,
That same old plaintive strain.
Hum, hum, hum, hum, hum,
That same old plaintive strain.

Hear that mournful melody,
It just haunts you the whole day long,
And you wander in dreams, back to Dixie, it seems,
When you hear that old song.
Hush a-bye, my baby, go to sleep on Mommy's knee,
Journey back to Dixieland in dreams again with me;
It seems like your Mommy is there again,
And the old folks were strummin' that old refrain.

Way down in Missouri where I learned this lullaby,
When the stars were blinkin' and the moon was climbin' high,
Seems I hear voices low, as in days long ago
Singin' hush a-bye.

STATE SONG: "MISSOURI WALTZ"

The "Missouri Waltz" was named the official state song in 1949. James Royce Shannon wrote the lyrics, and John Valentine Eppel wrote the music.

STATE FOLK DANCE: SQUARE DANCE

Missouri named the square dance its official state folk dance in 1995. Square dancing has been popular in Missouri since the **pioneer** days of the mid-1800s. Each wagon train heading west was required to have one dance caller and one fiddler.

The eastern bluebird has light blue feathers and a red breast that turns rust-colored in the fall.

STATE TREE: FLOWERING DOGWOOD

The flowering dogwood was named Missouri's official state tree in 1955. Each spring, people throughout the state see the dogwood in full bloom.

STATE BIRD: EASTERN BLUEBIRD

The eastern bluebird became Missouri's official bird on March 30, 1927. Bluebirds make their home all over Missouri from early spring until late November. Then they fly south for the winter.

STATE INSECT: HONEYBEE

The honeybee became Missouri's official state insect in 1985. The honeybee is common throughout Missouri. The sale of beeswax and honey contribute to the state's economy.

STATE ANIMAL: MISSOURI MULE

The Missouri mule was named the official state animal in 1995. It symbolizes Missourians' strength, intelligence, and healthy stubbornness.

The Missouri mule pulled many wagons west in the 1800s.

State Mineral: Galena

Galena is a chief source of lead. The selection of galena in 1967 as Missouri's official mineral symbolized the state's status as the number-one lead producer in the United States.

State Rock: Mozarkite

In 1967 mozarkite was named the official rock of Missouri. The name is a combination of Missouri ("Mo"), Ozarks ("zark"), and "ite," meaning rock. Mozarkite is a form of flint that is unique to Missouri. Its chief use is in decorative items, such as ornaments.

Galena is mined in the Joplin-Granby area in southwest Missouri.

State Fossil: Crinoid

The crinoid was named Missouri's official fossil in 1989. It is related to the starfish. It lived in the ocean that covered what is now Missouri 250 million years ago.

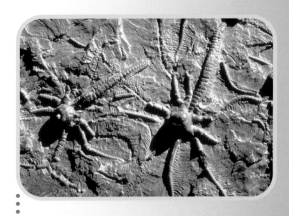

The crinoid is often called a "sea lily" because of its shape.

Missouri State Quarter

The Missouri state quarter shows explorers Meriwether Lewis and William Clark's return to St. Louis on the Missouri River after their journey to the Pacific Ocean. The Gateway Arch in St. Louis is shown in the background. The inscription on the quarter reads "Corps of Discovery 1804–2004." The dates mark the 200th anniversary of the trip.

Missouri's History and People

Missouri's history was shaped by a wide variety of people. From the ancient Native Americans to the first European settlers in the 1600s, Missouri has much to feel proud of and share with others.

THE EARLY CULTURE

A large population of an early Native American tribe called the Cahokia—frequently referred to as Mound Builders—lived in what is now the Missouri region since **prehistoric** times. Their society was at its peak from about 1050 to 1150. It is thought to have weakened around 1400, when fish supplies in the Mississippi River were dying due to the effects of soil **erosion.** The Cahokia built large earthen mounds that were likely used as burial grounds and also as the bases of temples. Some of the mounds are preserved throughout the state, but many were destroyed in the 1800s to make way for railroads.

The Missouri and Osage tribes lived in the area when European settlers arrived in the 1600s. By the 1820s settlers who wanted to control the land had driven most Native American tribes out of Missouri and moved them to Oklahoma.

FIRST EUROPEANS IN MISSOURI

In 1673 French explorers Louis Jolliet and Father Jacques Marquette marked the spot where the Missouri and Mississippi rivers join. Later, during the early to mid-1700s, more French settlers arrived and set up fur-trading posts along the rivers, started **missions,** and mined lead and salt. The first permanent European settlement in Missouri was founded at St. Genevieve, in 1735. French farmers and fur traders from across the Mississippi in Kaskasia, Illinois, had moved there.

THE LOUISIANA PURCHASE

The Territory of Missouri was part of the Louisiana Purchase—about 828,000 square miles of land—that President Thomas Jefferson had bought from France in 1803. This purchase tied the midwestern territories to those in the East.

Lewis and Clark's Expedition

On May 14, 1804, 28-year-old Meriwether Lewis and 32-year-old William Clark led a group from the U.S. Army on a journey to the West and back. President Thomas Jefferson wanted them to map the huge section of land he had bought in the interior of the continent. They were to follow the Missouri River west to the Pacific Ocean and the Columbia and Missouri rivers back to where they started. The Lewis and Clark Expedition returned to St. Louis in 1806. They covered about 8,000 miles of wilderness territory. They were gone for two years, four months, and nine days. Today, people visit the Lewis and Clark Center in St. Charles to celebrate and learn about these famous explorers.

The Civil War caused a great deal of difficulty to the families in Missouri. In many cases brother fought against brother in the Civil War. Today, many people remember the war by dressing in the uniforms of the day.

THE MISSOURI COMPROMISE AND STATEHOOD

By 1818 the United States had an equal number of slave and nonslave, or free, states. At the time, slavery was legal in slave states and illegal in free states. Whether a state was slave or free was up to each individual state to decide.

The U.S. Senate wanted to keep the balance of slave and free states so that both groups of states had equal representation in the Senate, or equal ability to vote for or against **legislation** as they wished. When Missouri, a slave territory, applied to become a state, it was a problem because adding another slave state to the Union would upset the balance. It would mean that slave states would have more power in the government.

That same year, Maine, a free territory, applied to become a state as well. This meant that both Missouri and Maine could be admitted without upsetting the balance of free and slave states. This led to the Missouri Compromise, a plan that admitted Maine as a free state. The people of Missouri voted to include slavery in their constitution, or plan of government. The compromise that Missouri made was accepting Congress's requirement that all Louisiana Purchase territory north of the southern boundary of Missouri, except Missouri itself, would be free. The territory below that line would be slave. Missouri became the 24th state on August 10, 1821.

MISSOURI IN THE CIVIL WAR

In the 1850s the Missouri-Kansas border was a battleground between people who wanted to preserve slavery and people who wanted to outlaw it. Both states had supporters on both sides of the issue.

The slavery issue led to war in 1861 between the states of the North, called the Union, and the states of the South, called the Confederacy because the Southern states wanted to form their own country. At first, Missouri could not decide whether to secede, or break away, from the Union and join the Confederacy. Governor Claiborne F. Jackson asked Missouri voters what they wanted to do. They voted to stay in the Union, even though several state leaders wanted to join the Confederacy.

In 1861 President Abraham Lincoln requested that Missouri troops report for fighting—on the Union side. Governor Jackson, who supported the Confederacy, refused and ordered his troops to fight Union soldiers. This started the first Civil War battle in the state. The Union quickly defeated Jackson's army and gained control of northern Missouri. In 1865 the war ended with a Union victory.

After the death of his father in 1847, Clemens began to work for a printer in Hannibal, where he learned the newspaper business.

FAMOUS PEOPLE FROM MISSOURI

Samuel Clemens (1835–1910), writer. Also known as Mark Twain, Clemens was born in the tiny town of Florida, Missouri. He grew up in the river town of Hannibal, where he spent countless hours watching the riverboats on the Mississippi River. Twain, who wrote in a unique plain-spoken style, is widely considered the greatest American **humorist.** His most popular books include *The Adventures of Tom Sawyer* and *The Adventures of Huckleberry Finn.*

George Washington Carver (1864–1943), scientist and educator. Carver was born into

At Iowa State, Carver was the only African American student.

slavery on a farm near Diamond. He graduated from Iowa State Agricultural College (now Iowa State University) in 1894. After earning a master's degree there in 1896, Carver accepted a teaching position at Tuskegee Institute (now Tuskegee University) in Alabama. Among other things, Carver was known for developing products such as soap, linoleum, and printer's ink from peanuts, and for creating products such as shoe polish and flour from sweet potatoes.

Harry S. Truman (1884–1972), politician. Perhaps Missouri's most famous person, Truman was born in Lamar. He served as a Jackson County judge, U.S. senator, and vice president before serving as the 33rd president of the United States (1945–1953). Truman took over as president just 83 days after becoming vice president, when Franklin D. Roosevelt died in office. At the time, the United States was involved in **World War II** (1939–1945) against Japan, Germany, and Italy. Truman made the decision to have American bombers drop the first atomic bombs over Hiroshima and Nagasaki, Japan, on August 6 and 9, 1945. Japan surrendered on September 2.

After serving his second term as president, Truman retired to his Independence home in 1953.

Thomas Hart Benton (1899–1975), artist. Benton was born in Neosho. One of his most famous works is a mural called *Independence and the Opening of the West* at the Truman Library in Independence. Its images include covered wagons, settlers, and Native Americans, illustrating the city's role in the nation's westward expansion.

Missouri-born artist Thomas Hart Benton was named for his great uncle, U.S. Senator Thomas Hart Benton, who served in Congress for 30 years (1821–1851).

Walt Disney (1901–1966), cartoon animator, film producer. Disney was born in Illinois, but he grew up in Missouri, first in Marceline and then St. Louis. In 1923 he moved from Kansas City to Hollywood to look for work in the film industry. He created Mickey Mouse in 1928 and went on to produce many classic animated movies, such as *Snow White and the Seven Dwarves, Pinocchio,* and *Bambi.* Walt Disney also created the theme parks Disneyland in Anaheim, California, and Walt Disney World near Orlando, Florida.

When Walt Disney showed his wife Lillian a sketch of Mortimer Mouse, Lillian suggested he name the character Mickey Mouse instead—and he took her advice!

Langston Hughes published his first book of poetry, The Weary Blues, *in 1926 when he was only 24 years old.*

Langston Hughes (1902–1967), writer. Born in Joplin, Hughes helped shape the literary movement known as the **Harlem Renaissance** during the 1920s. His writings focused attention on the African American experience. They explored street life in a section of New York City called Harlem, racial prejudice, poverty, love, and violence. Two of his most important works include the poem "I, Too," and the short story "Cora Unashamed."

Josephine Baker (1906–1975), entertainer. Baker was an internationally known African American singer and dancer. She was born in St. Louis and later moved to New York City to try to further her career. In 1925 Baker went from performing in New York nightclubs to the Paris stage, where she was wildly popular with audiences.

Josephine Baker was very popular in Paris and she loved it there. She retired from the stage in 1956 and became a French citizen.

In January 1993, Maya Angelou read an original poem at President Bill Clinton's inauguration ceremony.

Maya Angelou (1928–), writer. Born Marguerite Johnson, Maya Angelou hails from St. Louis. She went on to become a celebrated American poet, author, playwright, civil rights activist, and educator. Two of her best-known works are the books *I Know Why the Caged Bird Sings* and *Wouldn't Take Nothing for My Journey Now.*

Westward, Ho!

In the 1800s, **pioneers** were settling the American West. Missouri was a starting point for many journeys into these unknown lands because the Missouri and Mississippi rivers joined there. There were few good roads, and these rivers were used for trade and travel—much like the way highways are used today. That is why it made sense that sections of important overland trails began alongside the rivers in Missouri.

TRAILS WEST

The Santa Fe Trail played a big part in settling the West. It ran from Independence, Missouri, to today's Santa Fe, New Mexico, following an old Native American trail used for trade and travel. This route helped pioneers settle new areas, and it helped open up trade between the United States and Mexico. Many Missourians traveled to Santa Fe and traded their goods for Mexican mules and silver. This made many of them rich.

The Oregon-California trails served as paths to the California gold rush. In the mid-1800s, hundreds of thousands of Americans flocked west in search of one thing—gold. They had read about the available riches in newspapers. Some traveled by sea around

Many people traveled down the Santa Fe Trail in covered wagons.

23

South America. However, most pioneers joined wagon trains that followed the Oregon-California trails along the Missouri River. Fur trappers had created these paths in the 1820s. The first wagon train ever to travel the Oregon Trail left from Independence in 1841.

The busiest year of the California gold rush was 1849. That year, about 30,000 people seeking gold followed the trails from St. Joseph. The sometimes dangerous 2,000-mile trip to the Oregon and California goldfields usually took about five months. Travelers faced many hardships, such as lack of water, harsh weather, and disease.

The Pony Express

In the mid-1800s, news traveled slowly. In 1845 it took six months for a message from Washington, D.C., to reach California. In April 1860, a new mail service was born—the Pony Express. Riders on horseback carried mail from St. Joseph, Missouri, to Sacramento, California, and back again. A one-way trip took ten days—this was a big improvement! Riders and horses were changed often. There were about 100 **stations** along the route west, 80 riders, and 500 horses.

The Pony Express went out of business after eighteen months. The system worked well, but there was not enough money to keep it going.

Missouri's State Government

Missouri's state government is based in the state capital of Jefferson City. Missouri's constitution contains the rules for how the government should work. The government works much like the **federal government** and is divided into the same three branches: legislative, executive, and judicial.

THE LEGISLATIVE BRANCH

The legislative branch makes Missouri's laws by writing **bills,** voting on them, and passing approved bills on to the governor. This branch includes 34 members of the Senate and 163 members of the House of Representatives. Senators are elected to four-year terms, while House members serve two-year terms, or periods.

The present capitol was completed in 1917. It is the sixth capitol in Missouri's history

THE EXECUTIVE BRANCH

Missouri's executive branch is responsible for the state's daily business, such as ensuring that the laws of the state are carried out and managing the state budget. Missouri's governor heads this branch.

Missouri legislators debate whether to pass a bill.

The governor is elected by Missouri's voters to a four-year term and is responsible for reviewing bills passed by the legislative branch. The governor either signs a bill into law or **vetoes** it. The governor also creates Missouri's state budget.

Elected and appointed officials who work with the governor include the lieutenant governor, the secretary of state, and the attorney general. The lieutenant governor is president of the Missouri Senate and the official Elderly **Advocate** for the State of Missouri. The secretary of state oversees elections in Missouri and also is responsible for running several programs that benefit Missouri's citizens. One such program is the State Archives, which makes Missouri historical records and data available to the public. The attorney general is Missouri's chief **legal** officer. His or her job is to represent the legal interests of all state citizens as a group. The attorney general **prosecutes** those that break the laws of Missouri.

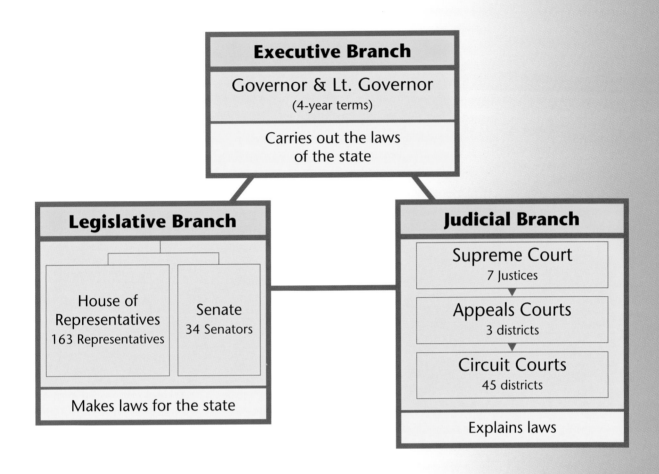

Executive Branch

Governor & Lt. Governor
(4-year terms)

Carries out the laws
of the state

Legislative Branch

House of Representatives
163 Representatives

Senate
34 Senators

Makes laws for the state

Judicial Branch

Supreme Court
7 Justices

Appeals Courts
3 districts

Circuit Courts
45 districts

Explains laws

JUDICIAL BRANCH

The judicial branch is the court system. The courts help interpret, or apply, Missouri's state laws. A case travels from one level to the next until a final decision is made. Lower court levels include 45 district circuit courts, also known as trial courts, and three district **appeals** courts. When Missouri's seven supreme court justices hear a case, that means the case has already been heard in one of the lower courts. The state supreme court has the final say in interpreting the law. The governor appoints Missouri's supreme court judges. After a judge serves one year, voters decide whether to keep him or her on the bench. After that, a judge then serves twelve-year terms and can continue to be reelected until he or she is 70 years old.

Missouri's Culture

Missouri has been called the "crossroads of the nation." This is because, during its early days, so many people from different cultural groups settled in Missouri or stopped through on their way to settle the West.

NATIVE AMERICAN CULTURE

Today, Native American groups such as the Sioux, Fox, and Cherokee live in Missouri. But during the 1800s, Missouri tribes, including the Fox, Osage, and Missouri, were forced to move to Oklahoma and other western territories by settlers who wanted their lands. The heritage of these Native Americans is celebrated at the Missouri State Powwow. This **intertribal** gathering is held each year at the Missouri State Fairgrounds in Sedalia. The event features Native American food, dancing, and arts and crafts such as paintings and silver jewelry.

EUROPEAN CULTURE

French explorers were the first Europeans to reach Missouri, arriving as far back as the 1600s. Visitors to the Soulard neighborhood in St. Louis can experience Missouri's French heritage. The neighborhood was named for a Frenchman who sur-

Visitors enjoy watching the authentic Native American dance performance at the Missouri State Powwow.

veyed the area for the king of Spain in the late 1700s. People enjoy shopping the outdoor Soulard Farmer's Market for fresh meats, spices, baked goods, vegetables, and flowers.

The historic Soulard Farmer's Market has been operating since 1838. Today, people from all over Missouri gather there to shop and listen to live music.

Missouri's earliest German communities date back to 1837 in Hermann and 1844 in Bethel. Today, the Historic Bethel German Colony and Hermann, "Missouri's Rhine Village," show visitors what these places were like in the mid-1800s. Every year in March, Hermann hosts Wurstfest, a festival that features sausage, a favorite German food.

HISPANIC CULTURE

Missouri's Hispanic roots can be traced to the 1840s, when wealthy Mexican traders brought their wagon trains to Kansas City on the Santa Fe Trail. Thousands of Hispanics settled in Missouri in the 1920s, and their communities thrive today. St. Louis hosts an annual Hispanic Festival in August, which celebrates Hispanic crafts, food, and music.

AFRICAN-AMERICAN CULTURE

African Americans have lived in Missouri since its earliest days as a territory. Many came as slaves as early as 1720, when Frenchman Philippe Francois Renault brought 500 slaves from Santo Domingo in the Dominican Republic to work in Missouri lead mines. African-American culture is celebrated during Kansas City's Black History Month Festival in February. The William Baker Festival Singers perform African-American spirituals and gospel songs.

Ozark Culture

The Missouri Ozarks are located in the south-central part of the state, and the area has its own cultural flavor.

Scottish, English, and Irish **immigrants** who had been farmers in Kentucky and Tennessee settled the Ozarks in the mid-1800s. They came to establish farming communities, and the area is still largely **rural** today. Far from city life and with few new people moving to the area, Ozarkers, or "hill people," established their own tightly knit culture. It celebrates traditional folktales, music, and dances from the first settlers' homelands.

The Missouri Folklore Society, based in Columbia, helps keep Ozark stories alive through exhibits, contests, and other events featuring storytelling. The folk music of the Ozarks often features instruments such as the fiddle, banjo, steel guitar, harmonica, and **dulcimer.** And the Ozark clogging tradition, in which dancers wearing wooden **clogs** tap or stamp in time to music, ensures that young people continue to learn the various forms of this dance.

There are about 10,000 natural springs in the Ozark Plateau.

Missouri's Food

Missourians and visitors alike enjoy everything from hearty meat-and-potatoes meals offered in the **Amish** community of Jamesport, to steaks and barbecue in Kansas City.

KANSAS CITY BARBECUE

Barbecuing involves roasting meat on a rack over hot coals or an open fire. Kansas City has been called the "Barbecue Capital of the World." Dozens of restaurants throughout the city are dedicated to the art of barbecue. There is even a club called the Kansas City Barbecue Society (KCBS). It has about 2,500 members worldwide and is the largest international organization of barbecue enthusiasts.

At Gates' Barbecue in Kansas City customers have their pick of many favorite dishes.

OTHER MISSOURI FOODS

Ozarkers eat meals such as fried catfish, cornbread, and peach cobbler. And in St. Louis, unique local Italian specialties include toasted ravioli and St. Louis-style, thin-crust pizza served in small square pieces. It is said that the thin crust and small pieces help the diner fully enjoy the fresh, flavorful toppings, which should be the focus of the dish.

Kansas City's Classic Barbecue Sauce

This sauce has all the tastes that Kansas City barbecue lovers expect to find in their special sauces. The brown sugar makes it slightly sweet, while the vinegar adds tang. You can use this as a dipping sauce for cut-up vegetables, or you can coat chicken or ribs with it before grilling.

Be sure to have an adult work the stovetop for you.

Ingredients

½ cup firmly packed dark brown sugar

1 tbsp onion salt

2 tsp garlic powder

2 tsp chili powder

2 tsp freshly ground black pepper

1 tsp celery seeds

1 tsp ground cumin

½ tsp cayenne pepper

2½ cups ketchup

⅓ cup white vinegar

2 tbsp prepared yellow mustard

1 tsp fresh lemon juice

1 tsp liquid smoke

3 tbsp butter, cubed and chilled

Directions

Combine all ingredients except the butter in a medium-sized saucepan. Bring to a boil over medium-high heat. Quickly stir mixture to dissolve the sugar. Reduce heat and simmer for 25 minutes, stirring frequently. Add the butter cubes, one at a time, and stir with a whisk. Makes about three cups.

Missouri's Folklore and Legends

Every state has its own unique set of folklore and legends, and Missouri is no exception. Folklore describes a culture's unique collection of traditional stories, or folktales. A folktale is a story meant to teach a lesson or explain an event, such as the creation of the world or why the sky is blue. A legend is also a traditional story. It is usually based on some factual information and often features historical characters. Many Missouri tales come from the Ozarks and Native American oral traditions. The Osage legend retold below explains how the Osage made earth their home.

CHILDREN OF THE SUN

Long ago, Osage Native Americans lived in the sky. They wanted to understand how they had gotten there, so they asked the mighty sun.

"Why, you are my children," said the sun. "I am your father."

"Who is our mother?" asked the Osage.

"I am your mother," replied the shimmering moon. "Now that you know where you came from, it is time for you to leave the sky. You must go now and live out your lives on earth."

The Osage did as they were told. When they got to earth, they found that it was covered with water. They did not

know what to do. They called out to the sun and the moon for help, but they received no answer.

To stay dry, the Osage floated above the water. They found that the animals were doing the same. Soon, they met an elk. He was a strong, brave animal.

"Can you help us?" the Osage asked the elk.

The elk said he would try. When he lowered himself into the water, he began to sink. The elk shouted, "Come and help us, wind!"

The wind appeared, blowing away some of the water so that the people and animals had dry land to walk upon.

The elk laughed and rolled around on the earth. Some of his hairs stuck in the dirt. Instantly, the hairs grew into grasses, trees, and food! There were potatoes, beans, and corn.

The Osage were happy to have a home on earth.

Missouri's Sports Teams

Professional athletic events such as baseball, football, and hockey draw large crowds in Missouri throughout the year.

RAMS AND CHIEFS

The St. Louis Rams play in the National Football League (NFL). Founded in 1937 as the Cleveland Rams, the team moved to Los Angeles in 1946 and St. Louis in 1995. The Rams had four straight losing seasons upon moving to St. Louis. However, led by quarterback Kurt Warner and running back Marshall Faulk, the team won the Super Bowl in 2000 and played in another in 2002.

Missouri's other NFL team is the Kansas City Chiefs. They play in Arrowhead Stadium. The Chiefs were originally based in Dallas, Texas, and known as the Texans. They moved to Kansas City and adopted their new name in 1963. The Chiefs played in two Super Bowls. They lost to the Green Bay Packers in the 1967 Super Bowl, but they defeated the Minnesota Vikings in the 1970 Super Bowl.

St. Louis Rams home football games take place in the Edward Jones Dome.

CARDINALS AND ROYALS

The St. Louis Cardinals major league baseball team plays in the National League. They play their home games at

The Royals play their home games at the Kauffman Stadium in Kansas City.

Busch Memorial Stadium in St. Louis. The Cardinals, originally called the Brown Stockings, or Browns, have been playing professional baseball since 1882. When the team's ownership changed, the team was called the Perfectos during the 1899 season. But fans called them the Cardinals because of the red trim on their uniforms. In 1900, the team's name was officially changed to the Cardinals.

Over the years, the Cardinals have won fifteen National League **pennants** and nine World Series titles. In 2000 and 2002 they won the Central Division championship. The Cardinals have had many great players. One of the most famous is first baseman Mark McGwire. He set a then major-league record in 1998 by hitting 70 home runs in one season.

The Kansas City Royals major league baseball team competes in the American League. Since they began in 1969, they have finished first or second in the Central Division during fourteen of their first twenty seasons. They have won two pennants and the 1985 World Series. Famous Royals have included third baseman George Brett and pitcher Dan Quisenberry.

The Blues

The St. Louis Blues hockey team came to Missouri in 1967. The Blues play in the Savvis Center. The team has enjoyed much success over the years. Between 1979 and 2000 they made it to the National Hockey League (NHL) playoffs 21 times in a row. Hockey greats that have played for the Blues include Brett Hull, Glenn Hall, Wayne Gretzky, and Peter Stastny.

Missouri's Businesses and Products

Missouri's businesses and products come from a unique blend of agriculture, mining, industry, and tourism.

AGRICULTURE

Missouri has about 110,000 farms that cover two-thirds of its land area. Beef cattle, hogs, and livestock products such as milk and eggs make up 60 percent of Missouri's farm income. Crops provide the other 40 percent of Missouri's agricultural income. The state's **fertile** soil and varied climate add up to an ideal farming environment. Missouri's main crops are soybeans, corn, and wheat.

MINING

Most of Missouri's annual mining **revenue** of $4.5 to $5 billion comes from lead, limestone, and coal. Missouri

Solving a Problem

At one time, the Boot Heel region, in the southeast corner of the state, was filled with forests and swampland. The state government decided to clear it so the land could be farmed. The land was drained and cleared around 1900. Streams were redug to straighten them for better drainage. Crops grown in the Boot Heel farmland include soybeans, rice, cotton, and melons.

The Old Lead Belt mining area in the Ozarks has many abandoned mines which are now flooded with water.

has been mining lead since 1720, and today it ranks first among the 50 states in lead production. Most mined lead is used in automobile batteries. Some of the biggest sources of lead in the world can be found in southeastern Missouri.

INDUSTRY

Missouri has always been an important industrial state. This is largely due to its location near the center of the United States and its position on the Missouri and Mississippi rivers, which makes getting to Missouri convenient for people nationwide. Major industries found throughout the state are manufacturing, transportation, health care, chemical production, food products, and real estate.

Well-known Missouri companies include Hallmark Cards, Ralston Purina, Boeing, and Monsanto. Founded in 1910 in Kansas City, Hallmark is the leading greeting card producer in the United States. It sells more than 3.5 billion cards per year. Pet-food producer Ralston Purina's headquarters are in St. Louis, and so is Boeing's military aircraft plant. The U.S. Air Force F-15 fighter plane is made in St. Louis. St. Louis-based Monsanto has been in business for more than 100 years. It is a global **biotechnology** company.

"Live Music Capital of the World"

Founded in 1903, Branson, which is located just south of Springfield, was once a sleepy little logging town. By the 1930s, visitors to Lake Taneycomo, Table Rock Lake, the White River, and other nearby waterways, had turned it into a popular vacation, or resort, town. Branson is now Missouri's biggest tourist draw and one of the most popular tourist spots in the United States, largely due to the busy music scene that earned Branson the nickname "Live Music Capital of the World." In 1959 Branson's first regular musical act, the Mabes Family, performed their mountain-music show *Ozarks Jubilee* using the City Hall basement as their theater. Today, about 65,000 visitors flock to Branson's 38 theaters every day to see musical acts that feature various styles of country-western music. Other types of entertainment found on the stages in Branson include jazz, rock 'n' roll, dance, and comedy.

TOURISM

Tourism in Missouri is a $12.76 billion industry. It employs about one in every fourteen people in the state. About 34 million people visit each year to take advantage of Missouri's lakes, mountains, caves, natural springs, state parks, and other outdoor wonders. People also visit Missouri for its historic sites, sporting events, festivals, and wide variety of cultural events.

Attractions and Landmarks

The following are some of the most popular places to visit in Missouri, listed roughly in the order you can find them when traveling the state from north to south.

PONY EXPRESS MUSEUM

The original Pony Express stables where riders took off for California still stand in St. Joseph. They are at the site of the Pony Express Museum. Visitors can see what it was like to choose a fresh horse, carry a Pony Express mailbag, send a telegraph, and set off on the Pony Express trail.

Mark Twain lived in this house from the time he was nine years old until he was eighteen years old.

MARK TWAIN BOYHOOD HOME AND MUSEUM

Located in Hannibal, Mark Twain's boyhood home and the museum next door let visitors take a peek at Aunt Polly's room, as described in *The Adventures of Tom Sawyer.* It also houses rare editions of Twain's books, and the pump organ he used to play. People can often be seen posing for photographs with statues of Twain's most beloved characters, Tom Sawyer and Huckleberry Finn.

Places to See in Missouri

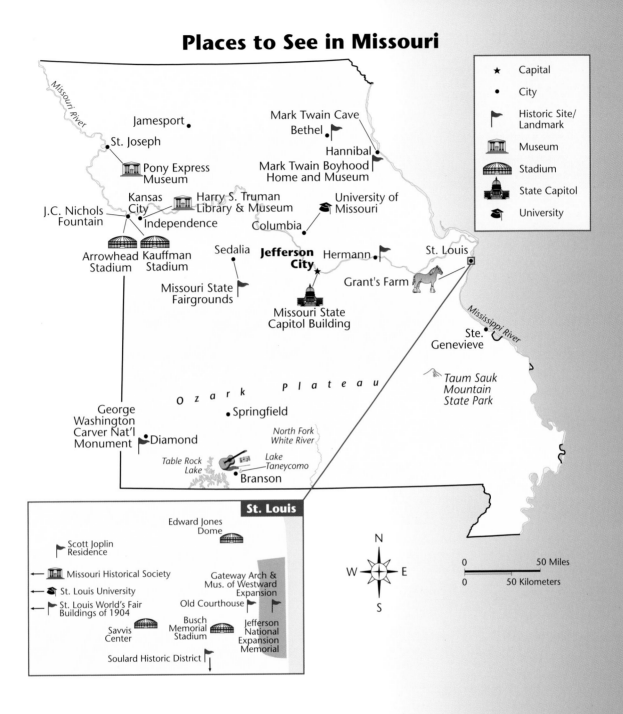

MARK TWAIN CAVE

Missouri has more than 1,450 caves. No other state has
as many. The caves are located in the Ozarks and were
formed by streams running underneath the mountains.
The Mark Twain Cave in Hannibal is the oldest tourist
cave in Missouri. People have been touring it for more
than 100 years.

The more than 5,000-ton arch was made mostly of stainless steel and cost about $15 billion to build.

GATEWAY ARCH

Built in 1965, the 630-foot-tall Gateway Arch is one of St. Louis's most popular attractions. The arch's foundation is buried 60 feet underground. This base helps steady the arch during high winds. The arch's width from the outside of each leg is 630 feet, or the length of nearly two football fields. Visitors can reach the observation deck, which can hold up to 140 people, by using one of two elevators or climbing 1,076 steps.

Scott Joplin's best-known songs include "The Maple Leaf Rag" and "The Entertainer."

SCOTT JOPLIN HOUSE

The Scott Joplin House in St. Louis is the onetime home of the famous African-American **ragtime** composer. It was built in the 1860s, and Joplin and his wife lived in an upstairs apartment from 1901 to 1903. Visitors can see Joplin's apartment and hear Joplin's music played on an antique player piano.

LEWIS AND CLARK: THE NATIONAL BICENTENNIAL EXHIBITION, MISSOURI HISTORICAL SOCIETY

This exhibit, opening in 2004 in St. Louis, celebrates the 200th anniversary of Lewis and Clark's journey through the American West. Visitors will learn about

The Jefferson National Expansion Memorial

Modern-day Missouri pays tribute to those who helped settle the West with the Jefferson National Expansion Memorial. The memorial includes the Gateway Arch, the Museum of Western Expansion, and the Old Courthouse of St. Louis. Visitors who look through the Arch's "gate" see a glimpse of the landscape **pioneers** saw, including the winding Mississippi River and rolling midwestern hills. The Museum of Western Expansion next to the Arch shows people what it was like for pioneers living in the 1800s. There visitors can see such unique **artifacts** as a chart of Lewis and Clark's famous journey west, a covered wagon, and a Native American tepee. The third part of the Memorial is the Old Courthouse, one of St. Louis's oldest buildings. Built in 1828, it is a museum of St. Louis history. People can learn about trials held there dating back to the 1840s.

Lewis and Clark's journey through maps, journals, artwork, and rare documents.

CLYDESDALE STABLES AT GRANT'S FARM

The Clydesdale Stables are at Grant's Farm, a wildlife preserve just south of St. Louis. Anheuser-Busch, Inc., owns

The Anheuser-Busch clydesdale farm has more than 250 horses, making it the largest clydesdale herd in the world.

the farm, which is home to the world-famous clydesdale horses. The clydesdale is known for being strong and large. The tip of the average male clydesdale's shoulder is more than six feet tall, and the horse can weigh up to 2,200 pounds. The clydesdale is also known for its coat, which typically is a deep brown with white markings across the horse's face and legs, and a black main and tail. Visitors to the Clydesdale Stables can tour the stables and also watch shows featuring the magnificent clydesdales.

GEORGE WASHINGTON CARVER NATIONAL MONUMENT

This memorial park near Diamond in southwestern Missouri includes the cabin where Carver was born, a family cemetery, and a nature trail. The Carver Science Discovery Center is also part of the park. Here student groups can use the scientific equipment to conduct experiments related to Carver's work in nutrition, soil science, and other areas.

HARRY S. TRUMAN LIBRARY AND MUSEUM

Located in Independence, the library and museum offer many **artifacts** from Truman's boyhood in Independence, his political life, and his life after leaving public office. The museum features such items as Truman's canes and hats, books, paintings that hung in the White House, and political buttons.

Map of Missouri

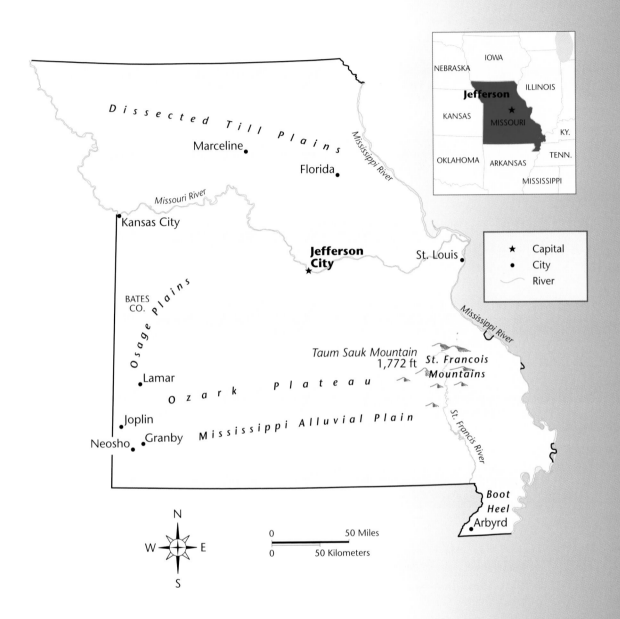

IOWA
NEBRASKA
ILLINOIS
Jefferson
KANSAS
★
MISSOURI
KY.
OKLAHOMA
ARKANSAS
TENN.
MISSISSIPPI

Dissected Till Plains

Marceline

Florida

Mississippi River

Missouri River

Kansas City

Jefferson City
★

St. Louis

Mississippi River

★ Capital
• City
⌇ River

BATES CO.

Osage Plains

Taum Sauk Mountain
1,772 ft

St. Francois Mountains

Lamar

Ozark Plateau

Joplin

Mississippi Alluvial Plain

Neosho • Granby

St. Francis River

Boot Heel
Arbyrd

N
W E
S

0   50 Miles
0   50 Kilometers

45

Glossary

advocate one who acts on behalf of a person, group, or cause

Amish religious group who moved to the United States in the eighteenth century

appeals formal requests to a higher court requesting either a change in or confirmation of a decision

artifacts historical objects

bills written proposals for new laws

biotechnology the use of living organisms or biological substances to perform certain industrial or manufacturing processes

blues musical style that grew out of African American folk music in the early 20th century and often features slow, sad songs

charter official document that recognizes the formation of an organization or school

clogs shoes with thick wooden soles

cumulonimbus cloud tall, dark cloud that often produces thunderstorms

dulcimer boxy, guitar-like stringed instrument played with a hammer or by plucking

erosion gradual wearing away of rock or soil caused by water, wind, or ice

federal government United States government in Washington, D.C.

fertile full of nutrients needed to produce crops and other plants

guerrilla soldier group organized outside the official military

Harlem Renaissance period from about 1915 through the mid-1930s, during which a group of African American writers produced important works of literature

humidity condition of having a high amount of moisture in the air

humorist one who writes or performs works of comedy

immigrants people who move to a new country and settle there

intertribal involving two or more tribes

journalism profession of gathering and reporting news

legal having to do with laws and rules

legislation laws passed by a government body

metropolitan including the large area and nearby communities surrounding a city

missions places where a religious group teaches its beliefs

murals large scenes painted directly onto a wall

pennants championship flags

pioneers people who lead the way to a new place or information

prairie grass-covered plain in the midwestern United States

prehistoric before recorded history

prosecutes to bring legal action against someone for breaking a law

ragtime popular American musical style of the late nineteenth and early twentieth centuries that featured unusual rhythms

ready-mix mix that contains the correct blend of ingredients—such as flour, sugar, salt, and baking powder—so cooks can prepare the food quickly and easily

revenue money earned from a business or government's sale of goods and services

rural typical of country and farm life

stations stopping place along a route

terrain piece of land evaluated in terms of its physical features

veto right of a chief executive, such as a governor or a president, to reject a law passed by lawmakers

World War II a war fought from 1939 to 1945 in which Great Britain, France, the Soviet Union, the United States, and their allies defeated Germany, Italy, and Japan.

More Books to Read

· ·

Ingram, Scott. Missouri: *The Show-Me State.* New York: World Almanac Education, 2002.

Johmann, Carol A. *The Lewis and Clark Expedition.* Charlotte, VT: Williamson Publishing, 2002.

Kummer, Patricia K. *Missouri.* Mankato, MN: Capstone Press, 2003.

Sandweiss, Lee Ann. *St. Louis Architecture for Kids.* St. Louis: Missouri Historical Society, 2001.

Index

About the Author

Lisa Owens grew up in the Midwest and currently lives near Chicago, Illinois. She has written more than 25 books for children and especially loves writing about unique places such as Missouri. A frequent visitor to Missouri, she counts the beautiful Ozarks and the cities of St. Louis and Kansas City as some of her favorite spots.